UNVEILING

MALAGA

Your Travel Guide to Andalusia's Coastal Crown

presented by

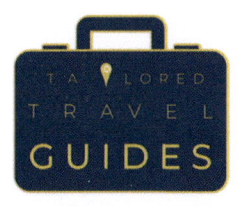

TAILORED TRAVEL GUIDES

Discover your journey!

Presented by Tailored Travel Guides
a WEST AGORA INT S.R.L. Brand
www.tailoredtravelguides.com

Edited by WEST AGORA INT S.R.L.
WEST AGORA INT S.R.L. All Rights Reserved
Copyright © WEST AGORA INT S.R.L., 2023

CONTENTS

1 — GREETINGS AND RECOMMENDATIONS FROM LOCALS

PRACTICAL INFORMATION — 2

6 — TOP ATTRACTIONS IN MALAGA

HIDDEN GEMS AND LESSER-KNOWN SIGHTS IN MALAGA — 10

13 — PARKS AND GARDENS IN MALAGA

MALAGA'S CULINARY SCENE — 15

17 — SHOPPING IN MALAGA

FAMILY-FRIENDLY ACTIVITIES IN MALAGA — 19

21 — MALAGA BY NIGHT

ART AND CULTURE IN MALAGA — 27

30 — HISTORICAL AND ARCHITECTURAL LANDMARKS IN MALAGA

DAY TRIPS FROM MALAGA — 33

35 — END NOTE

MALAGA

ANDALUSIA'S COASTAL CROWN

Málaga, the Coastal Jewel of Andalusia
Perched along the sun-drenched Costa del Sol, Málaga radiates the allure of Spain's diverse heritage. This maritime city, bathed in Mediterranean hues, narrates tales of Phoenician traders, Roman theaters, and Moorish citadels. The grandeur of the Alcazaba fortress, combined with the city's golden beaches and verdant gardens, positions Málaga as a mosaic of historical depth and modern vibrancy.

The Symphony of Seaside Splendor and Andalusian Tradition
Málaga's lively ferias dance to the rhythm of flamenco guitars, harmonizing with the gentle whispers of the sea. As the birthplace of Picasso, the city's artistic spirit is palpable, from its renowned museums to the colorful murals that adorn its streets. The aroma of grilled sardines, fresh from the sea, mingles with the sweet scent of Malaga wine, encapsulating the city's gastronomic delights. As dusk descends, the Gibralfaro castle casts a shadow over the bustling port, recounting legends of ancient mariners and age-old voyages.

Your Gateway to the Essence of Coastal Andalusia
This guide is your compass to navigate Málaga's treasures. From the intricate halls of the Picasso Museum to the bustling atmosphere of Atarazanas Market, from the historic Roman Theatre to the serene beauty of the Concepción Botanical Garden, we beckon you to traverse these pages and uncover Málaga's soul. Whether you're captivated by its maritime history, culinary adventures, or the melodic waves crashing on its shores, Málaga promises a captivating tale for every wanderer.

GREETINGS AND
INSIGHTS FROM LOCALS

¡Bienvenido, dear traveler! Welcome to Málaga, where the Mediterranean whispers tales of ancient mariners and modern merriment. As a Malagueño, the rhythmic pulse of this coastal haven has always echoed in my heart, and I am thrilled to unveil treasures that only a true local would know.

Embark on your Malagan journey by immersing yourself in our warm embrace of tradition. A sincere "hola" paired with our sun-infused olives can be your key to the city's soul, guiding you through Roman amphitheaters, Moorish castles, and vibrant boulevards kissed by Picasso's genius.

Perhaps the maze-like streets of the Historic Centre will beckon. Here, in Málaga's heart, every stone and balcony narrates tales of Phoenicians and Moors, harmonizing gracefully with the city's contemporary zest.

For an artsy detour, don't miss the Pompidou Centre. This Parisian transplant, with its colorful cube emblem, houses avant-garde masterpieces, adding a modern brushstroke to Málaga's rich canvas of history.

When the sea breeze kindles your appetite, navigate to Atarazanas Market where you can relish Malagan delicacies from freshly caught sardines to aromatic wines. Our crowning glory? Espetos de sardinas – grilled sardines skewered on bamboo, a taste that embodies the spirit of our shores.

As the golden hour bathes Málaga, find solace by the Malagueta Beach. Here, silhouettes of playful families and tranquil tides craft a panorama of life and leisure.

Standing tall amidst this landscape, the Málaga Cathedral invites you with open arms. A marvel of Renaissance architecture, its incomplete tower adds a touch of mystery to its majesty, symbolizing Málaga's ever-evolving journey.

As you traverse Málaga, let its mosaic of old-world charm and new-age vibrancy serenade you. We, the Malagueños, with sand in our shoes and stories in our eyes, are eager to share the enchantment of our seaside sanctuary. ¡Hasta pronto, dear traveler, and may your Malagan memories shimmer with the brilliance of our Mediterranean sun!

PRACTICAL INFORMATION

Currency
Spain uses the Euro (€) as its currency. In Malaga, credit cards are commonly accepted in most establishments, including restaurants and larger shops. However, when visiting smaller boutiques, local eateries, or market stalls, it's a good idea to have some cash on hand.

Transportation
Malaga is well-connected with an efficient public transportation system. The city's buses and trains are operated by EMT (Empresa Malagueña de Transportes). The Malaga Metro is a light metro network serving the city and its suburbs.

Driving in Malaga
Driving is on the right side of the road. Parking can be challenging in the city center, so it's advisable to use public transport or park in designated parking areas.

Language
Spanish is the official language. However, English is widely spoken in tourist areas.

Power sockets and adapters
Spain uses Type F power sockets. The standard voltage is 230 V, and the standard frequency is 50 Hz. Travelers from countries with different socket types might need an adapter.

Shopping
Malaga offers a mix of traditional shops selling local crafts and modern shopping malls. The city is known for its ceramics, hand-embroidered shawls, and gourmet foods.

Tipping
Tipping is not mandatory in Spain, but it's customary to leave a small tip (around 5-10%) for good service in restaurants and cafes.

PRACTICAL INFORMATION

USEFUL LINKS AND PHONE NUMBERS

Emergency Services
All Emergencies: 112
Police: 091
Fire Brigade: 080
Medical Emergencies: 061

Transportation
Malaga Airport: +34 952 04 88 04, www.aena.es/en/malaga-costa-del-sol.html
Renfe (Spanish National Railway Company): +34 912 320 320, www.renfe.com/es/en
EMT (Public Transport in Malaga): +34 902 527 200, www.emtmalaga.es

Tourist Information
Malaga Tourism Office: +34 951 926 020, https://visita.malaga.eu/en/
Tourist Map www.ontheworldmap.com/spain/city/malaga/malaga-tourist-map.jpg

Hospitals
Hospital Universitario Regional de Málaga, Address: Avenida del Doctor Gálvez Ginachero, s/n, 29009 Málaga, Spain, Phone: +34 951 29 01 00 http://www.hospitalregionaldemalaga.es/

Local Government
City of Malaga: +34 951 926 010, www.malaga.eu

Maps
Malaga maps: www.ontheworldmap.com/spain/city/malaga/
Malaga Street Map: www.ontheworldmap.com/spain/city/malaga/malaga-street-map.jpg
Malaga Tourist Map: www.ontheworldmap.com/spain/city/malaga/malaga-tourist-map.jpg
Malaga Bus Map: www.ontheworldmap.com/spain/city/malaga/malaga-bus-map.jpg
Malaga Metro: www.ontheworldmap.com/spain/city/malaga/malaga-metro-map.jpg

PRACTICAL INFORMATION
MALAGA GENERAL MAP

MÁLAGA
PLANO CENTRO HISTÓRICO

INFORMACIÓN TURÍSTICA
FERROCARRIL
ESTACIÓN AUTOBUSES
TAXI
APARCAMIENTO

Free high resolution download at: www.ontheworldmap.com/spain/city/malaga/malaga-street-map.jpg

PRACTICAL INFORMATION
MALAGA BUSS MAP

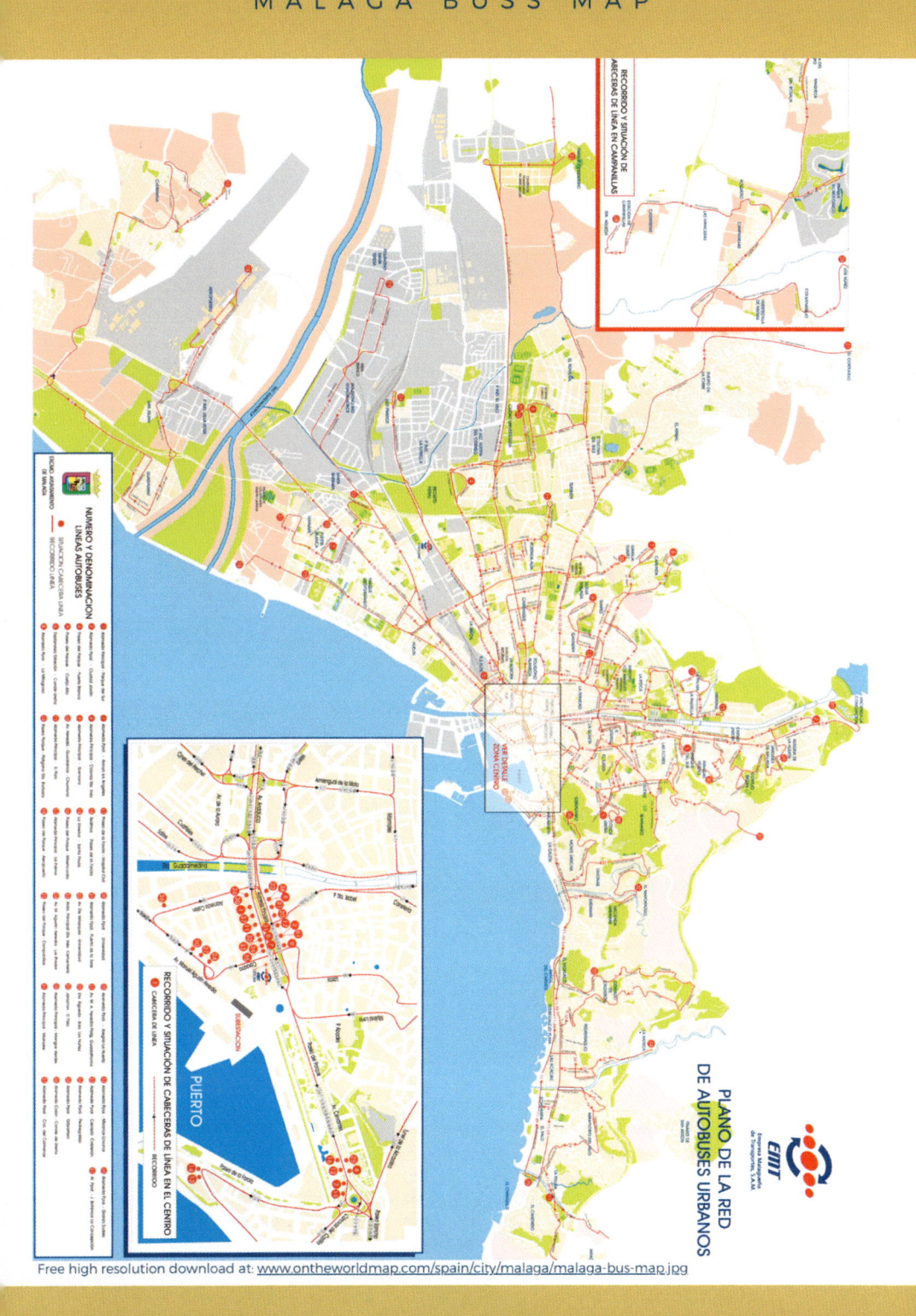

TOP ATTRACTIONS IN MALAGA

ALCAZABA OF MALAGA

The Alcazaba of Malaga is a testament to the city's rich Moorish history. Built in the 11th century, this palatial fortification stands majestically atop a hill, offering panoramic views of the city and the azure Mediterranean Sea. As you wander through its labyrinthine corridors and ascend its towering ramparts, you'll be transported back in time, with its beautifully preserved archways, courtyards, and fountains. The lush gardens, adorned with exotic plants and bubbling fountains, offer a tranquil retreat, echoing tales of sultans and poets from bygone eras. The Alcazaba is not just a historical monument but a symbol of Malaga's enduring spirit, resilience, and cultural confluence.

Website: www.alcazabamalaga.com
Location: Calle Alcazabilla, 2, 29012 Málaga, Spain
Tip: To truly appreciate its beauty, visit during sunset when the golden hues bathe the fortress in a magical glow, and the city lights begin to twinkle below.

PICASSO MUSEUM

Born in Malaga in 1881, Pablo Picasso is undoubtedly the city's most illustrious son and a towering figure in 20th-century art. The Picasso Museum, gracefully housed in the Renaissance-style Palacio de Buenavista, stands as a tribute to the artist's prodigious legacy. With over 200 works meticulously curated, the museum offers a comprehensive overview of Picasso's artistic evolution, tracing his journey from his formative years to his avant-garde explorations. Each room unravels a chapter, shedding light on the different phases of his life, the societal influences, and the personal experiences that molded his art. The museum not only showcases his masterpieces but also provides glimpses into his personal life, relationships, and the vibrant epochs he lived through. Whether you're an art connoisseur or a curious traveler, the Picasso Museum offers an immersive journey into the creative universe of a genius.

Website: www.museopicassomalaga.org/en
Location: Palacio de Buenavista, C. San Agustín, 8, 29015 Málaga, Spain
Tip: Audio guides are available and offer valuable insights into Picasso's life, his inspirations, and the intricate nuances of his works.

TOP ATTRACTIONS IN MALAGA

MALAGA CATHEDRAL

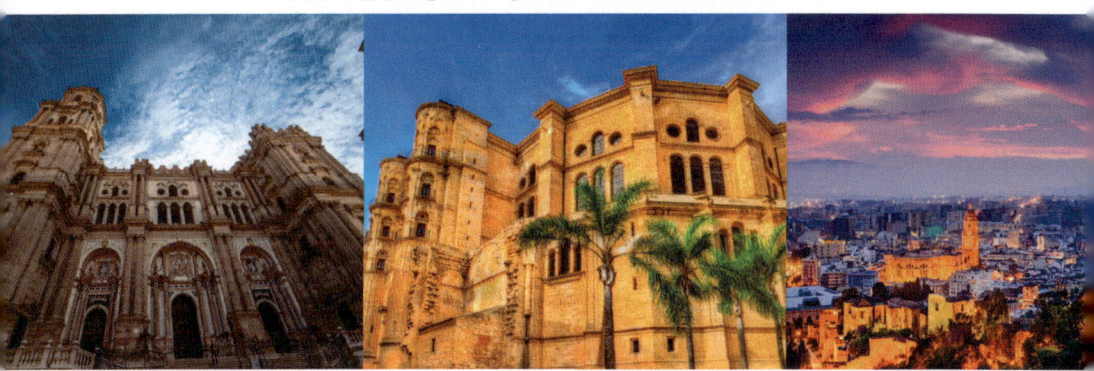

Dominating Malaga's skyline, the Malaga Cathedral, also known as "La Manquita" or "The One-Armed Lady", is a marvel of Renaissance architecture. Constructed between the 16th and 18th centuries, the cathedral boasts a stunning façade, intricate stained glass windows, and a grand interior adorned with sculptures and paintings. The north tower stands tall at 84 meters, while the south tower remains unfinished, giving the cathedral its unique nickname. Climb to the rooftop for a bird's-eye view of the city and the azure Mediterranean Sea.
Website: www.malagacatedral.com
Location: Calle Molina Lario, 9, 29015 Málaga, Spain
Tip: The cathedral's choir stalls, carved from mahogany and cedar, are considered one of the finest examples of Spanish Baroque woodcarving.

MUELLE UNO

Muelle Uno is Málaga's modern waterfront development, offering a blend of shopping, dining, and entertainment. With views of the Alcazaba and the Gibralfaro Castle, it's a scenic place to stroll, shop, or simply relax by the Mediterranean Sea. The area also hosts various events, from markets to concerts, adding to its vibrant atmosphere.
Website: www.muelleuno.com
Location: Paseo del Muelle Uno, 29016 Málaga, Spain
Tip: Visit during sunset for a picturesque view of the city's landmarks against the backdrop of the setting sun.

TOP ATTRACTIONS IN MALAGA

AUTOMOBILE AND FASHION MUSEUM

A unique combination of vintage cars and haute couture, the Automobile and Fashion Museum is a treat for both car enthusiasts and fashion lovers. The museum showcases a collection of over 90 classic cars, each paired with fashion pieces from the same era, illustrating the evolution of design in both fields throughout the 20th century.
Website: https://museoautomovilmalaga.com/
Location: Avenida de Sor Teresa Prat, 15, 29003 Málaga, Spain
Tip: Don't miss the thematic areas, which delve into specific periods, from the Roaring Twenties to the Swinging Sixties.

BEACHES OF MALAGA

Malaga's coastline boasts a diverse range of beaches, each with its own unique charm. La Malagueta, the city's most iconic beach, is known for its urban setting and lively atmosphere. Pedregalejo, with its traditional fishing boats and old-world charm, offers a glimpse into Malaga's maritime heritage. Playa de la Caleta is favored for its calm waters and palm-lined promenade, making it perfect for families. El Palo, once a traditional fishing village, retains its authentic charm with numerous seafood restaurants lining its shores. Whether you're looking for bustling beach activities or a serene spot to relax, Malaga's beaches cater to every preference.
Website: https://visita.malaga.eu/en/what-to-see-and-do/beaches
Location: Malaga's Coastal Line, Malaga, Spain
Tip: For a traditional experience, try 'espetos' – sardines skewered and grilled over open fires, a local delicacy available at many beachside chiringuitos.

TOP ATTRACTIONS IN MALAGA

LA CONCEPCIÓN HISTORICAL-BOTANICAL GARDENS

A lush tropical paradise awaits visitors at La Concepción Historical-Botanical Gardens. Established in the mid-19th century, this garden is home to over 2,000 species of plants from five continents. Wander through the romantic-style gardens, discover waterfalls, and marvel at the ancient trees. The garden also offers spectacular views of Málaga, making it a serene escape from the city's hustle and bustle.
Website: www.laconcepcion.malaga.eu/en/index.html
Location: Cam. del Jardin Botanico, 3, 29014 Málaga, Spain
Tip: The garden hosts seasonal events and workshops. Check their calendar for any special happenings during your visit.

PLAZA DE TOROS DE LA MALAGUETA

Situated close to the Malagueta beach, the Plaza de toros de La Malagueta is one of Malaga's iconic landmarks. This historic bullring, built in the 19th century, showcases neo-Mudejar architecture and has witnessed countless thrilling bullfights over the years. While bullfighting remains a contentious topic, the arena itself stands as a testament to Andalusian culture and tradition. Even if you're not attending a bullfight, the attached museum offers insights into the history and artistry of this age-old spectacle.
Website: www.plazadetoroslamalagueta.com/en/
Location: Paseo de Reding, 8, 29016 Málaga, Spain
Tip: The museum inside provides a deeper understanding of the cultural significance of bullfighting in Spain.

PLAZA DE LA MERCED

Plaza de la Merced is one of Malaga's most lively and historic squares. Dominated by the towering obelisk commemorating General Torrijos, the plaza is surrounded by colorful buildings and bustling terraces. It's a hub of activity, with street performers, local artists, and vendors adding to its vibrant atmosphere. Notably, it's also the birthplace of Pablo Picasso, with his childhood home now transformed into the Fundación Picasso museum. Whether you're sipping a coffee at a local café, admiring the surrounding architecture, or simply people-watching, Plaza de la Merced encapsulates the spirit of Malaga.
Website: https://visita.malaga.eu/en/things-to-do/plaza-de-la-merced-mercy-square-p103360
Location: Plaza de la Merced, 29012 Málaga, Spain
Tip: Don't miss the Picasso statue seated on a bench in the square – a perfect photo opportunity for art enthusiasts.

HIDDEN GEMS AND LESSER-KNOWN SIGHTS IN MALAGA

LA CASA INVISIBLE

Tucked away in the heart of Málaga, La Casa Invisible is a cultural community center that offers a diverse range of workshops, events, and exhibitions. From art and music to politics and ecology, this space is a hub for alternative and creative thinking.

Website: http://lainvisible.net/
Location: Calle Andrés Pérez, 8, 29008 Málaga, Spain
Tip: Check their calendar for any ongoing events or workshops during your visit. It's a great way to immerse yourself in the local culture.

ENGLISH CEMETERY

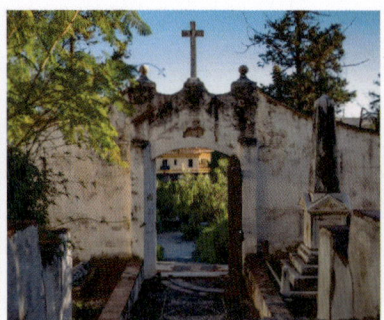

A serene oasis in the city, the English Cemetery is the final resting place for many non-Catholic foreigners who made Málaga their home. With its lush greenery, historic tombs, and peaceful ambiance, it's a reflective spot to wander and learn about the city's diverse past.
Website: www.cementerioinglesmalaga.org/en/
Location: Avenida de Pries, 1, 29016 Málaga, Spain
Tip: Take a guided tour to delve deeper into the stories of the individuals buried here and the cemetery's significance in Málaga's history.

MERCADO DE LA MERCED

While the Plaza de la Merced is well-known, the nearby Mercado de la Merced is a lesser-explored gem. This bustling market offers a plethora of fresh produce, meats, cheeses, and more. It's a sensory delight and a glimpse into the daily life of locals.
Website:
www.mercadomalaga.es/mercados/mercado-de-la-merced/
Location: Calle Merced, 4, 29012 Málaga, Spain
Tip: Visit in the morning when the market is most lively. Don't forget to sample some local cheeses and olives!

HIDDEN GEMS AND LESSER-KNOWN SIGHTS IN MALAGA

LA TERMICA CULTURAL CENTER

Once an old hospital, La Termica has been transformed into a vibrant cultural center. It hosts a myriad of events, workshops, and exhibitions throughout the year, ranging from contemporary art to music and theater. The architecture alone, with its blend of old and new, makes it worth a visit. The center also has a lovely café where you can relax and soak in the ambiance.

Website: www.latermicamalaga.com
Location: Avenida de los Guindos, 48, 29004 Málaga, Spain
Tip: The center often hosts free events, so check their calendar in advance. The outdoor garden area is a peaceful spot to unwind.

ATARAZANAS MARKET

While many tourists flock to the city's main attractions, Atarazanas Market remains a bit off the beaten path. This bustling market is housed in a historic building with a stunning stained glass window. Inside, you'll find a plethora of stalls selling fresh produce, meats, seafood, and local delicacies. The sights, sounds, and smells are a feast for the senses, offering a genuine taste of Málaga's vibrant culinary scene.

Website: www.mercadomalaga.es/en/markets/central-market-atarazanas/
Location: Calle Atarazanas, 10, 29005 Málaga, Spain
Tip: Try the freshly squeezed orange juice from one of the stalls, and if you're a seafood lover, don't miss the chance to sample some boquerones (anchovies) – a local favorite.

TEATRO ROMANO (ROMAN THEATRE)

Tucked away at the foot of the Alcazaba fortress, the Teatro Romano is one of Malaga's most treasured archaeological sites. Dating back to the 1st century BC, this ancient theatre has witnessed countless performances over the centuries. Though it lay buried and forgotten for many years, recent excavations have brought its grandeur back to life. Today, visitors can explore its semicircular orchestra, tiered seating, and stage while imagining the theatrical spectacles that once captivated audiences. The adjacent interpretation center offers deeper insights into its history and significance. A visit to the Teatro Romano is a journey back in time, offering a glimpse into Malaga's rich Roman heritage.

Website: www.andalucia.com/cities/malaga/teatro-romano.htm
Location: Calle Alcazabilla, s/n, 29015 Málaga, Spain
Tip: Combine your visit with the Alcazaba for a comprehensive understanding of Malaga's ancient history. The theatre occasionally hosts live performances, offering a unique experience in a historic setting.

HIDDEN GEMS AND LESSER-KNOWN SIGHTS IN MALAGA

GIBRALFARO CASTLE

While the Alcazaba often takes the spotlight, the Castillo de Gibralfaro, perched high above the city, is a lesser-visited treasure. This Moorish fortress dates back to the 10th century and offers panoramic views of Málaga and the Mediterranean Sea. The castle walls, towers, and ramparts are well-preserved, allowing visitors to step back in time and imagine the historical events that took place here.

Website: https://alcazabaygibralfaro.malaga.eu/en/index.html
Location: Cam. Gibralfaro, 11, 29016 Málaga, Spain
Tip: Visit in the early morning or late afternoon to avoid the midday sun. The walk uphill can be strenuous, but the views are worth the effort.

MUSEO CARMEN THYSSEN MÁLAGA

Nestled in a 16th-century palace, the Carmen Thyssen Museum is a haven for art enthusiasts. It boasts an impressive collection of 19th-century Spanish paintings, with a particular focus on Andalusian art. The museum offers a journey through Spain's artistic evolution, from romantic landscapes to vibrant Andalusian scenes. Temporary exhibitions further enrich the museum's offerings.

Website: www.carmenthyssenmalaga.org
Location: Calle Compañía, 10, 29008 Málaga, Spain **Tip**: The museum's courtyard café is a delightful spot to relax and reflect on the artworks you've seen.

MUSEO DE MÁLAGA (MÁLAGA MUSEUM)

Nestled within the grandeur of the Palacio de la Aduana, the Museo de Málaga is a treasure trove of art and archaeology. While it may not be as internationally renowned as some of the city's other institutions, it boasts an impressive collection of over 15,000 archaeological artifacts and 2,000 fine art pieces. The museum beautifully chronicles the region's rich tapestry of history, from its Phoenician roots to its Roman, Moorish, and Christian eras. The art section showcases works from the 19th and 20th centuries, reflecting the cultural and societal shifts of the times. The Museo de Málaga is a quiet sanctuary for those seeking to delve deeper into the city's multifaceted heritage.

Website: www.carmenthyssenmalaga.org
Location: Plaza de la Aduana, s/n, 29015 Málaga, Spain
Tip: The museum offers free entry to EU citizens, and its serene courtyards are perfect for a reflective pause during your exploration. Don't miss the intricate mosaics and the collection of ancient coins.

PARKS AND GARDENS IN MALAGA

PARQUE DEL OESTE (WEST PARK)

A verdant oasis in the heart of the city, Parque del Oeste offers a refreshing escape from the urban hustle. This expansive park is a harmonious blend of manicured gardens, meandering pathways, and serene ponds. Sculptures dot the landscape, adding an artistic touch to the natural beauty. Children can delight in the playground areas, while adults find solace in the shaded corners, perfect for relaxation or a leisurely read. The park's diverse flora, ranging from palm trees to exotic plants, creates a tropical ambiance that captivates visitors.
Website: www.malaga.es/en/laprovincia/naturaleza/lis_cd-3727/parque-del-oeste
Location: Av. de Manuel Agustín Heredia, 29002 Málaga, Spain
Tip: The park often hosts cultural events and fairs, so keep an eye out for local happenings during your visit.

PARQUE DE LA PALOMA

Situated in Benalmádena, a short distance from Málaga, Parque De La Paloma is a sprawling green haven known for its picturesque landscapes and diverse fauna. The park is home to a variety of animals, including rabbits, peacocks, and ducks, freely roaming the grounds. With its large lake, cascading waterfalls, and cactus garden, the park offers a myriad of scenic spots. Children's play areas, picnic zones, and open spaces make it a favorite among families. The well-maintained trails are ideal for both leisurely strolls and invigorating jogs.
Website: www.andalucia.org/en/visitas-parque-de-la-paloma
Location: Av. Federico García Lorca, s/n, 29630 Benalmádena, Málaga, Spain
Tip: Don't forget to visit the park's cactus garden, which boasts an impressive collection of cacti and succulents from around the world.

PARQUE DE MÁLAGA (MÁLAGA PARK)

Stretching along the city's main boulevard, this park is a green oasis amidst Málaga's urban landscape. With its fountains, sculptures, and exotic plants, it's a favorite spot for both locals and tourists. The park is a testament to Málaga's rich history, with monuments and plaques detailing significant events.
Website: www.spain.info/en/places-of-interest/malaga-park/
Location: Paseo del Parque, 29016 Málaga, Spain
Tip: The park is beautifully illuminated in the evenings, making it a romantic spot for a nighttime stroll.

PARKS AND GARDENS IN MALAGA

MONTES DE MÁLAGA NATURAL PARK

Just a short drive from the city, this natural park offers a refreshing escape into nature. With its pine forests, hiking trails, and panoramic viewpoints, it's a haven for nature lovers. The park is also home to diverse wildlife, including foxes, wild boars, and various bird species.
Website: www.andalucia.org/en/natural-spaces-montes-de-malaga
Location: Montes de Málaga, 29013 Málaga, Spain
Tip: Visit the Ecomuseum to learn about the park's ecology and the traditional ways of life in the Montes de Málaga.

JARDINES DE PEDRO LUIS ALONSO

A tribute to the modernist style, these gardens are a harmonious blend of French, Arab, and Andalusian designs. Lined with orange trees, rose bushes, and fountains, the gardens offer a tranquil space in the heart of the city. The geometric patterns and symmetrical designs are reminiscent of the Alhambra's Generalife gardens.
Website: https://visita.malaga.eu/es/que-ver-y-hacer/visitas/monumentos-historicos/parques-y-jardines-historicos/jardines-de-pedro-luis-alonso-p103353
Location: C. Guillén Sotelo, 31, 29016 Málaga, Spain
Tip: The gardens are adjacent to the Málaga Town Hall, another architectural gem worth exploring.

PARQUE DE LAS CIENCIAS

Nestled on the slopes of Mount Gibralfaro, these terraced gardens offer a multi-level experience. As you ascend, you'll find a variety of plants, from tropical species at the base to native Mediterranean flora at the top. The gardens also provide stunning views of the Alcazaba and the city below.
Website: https://visita.malaga.eu/es/que-ver-y-hacer/visitas/monumentos-historicos/parques-y-jardines-historicos/jardines-de-puerta-oscura-p103354
Location: Pl. Jardín de San Antonio, 29016 Málaga, Spain
Tip: The gardens are a great spot to relax after visiting the nearby Alcazaba and Gibralfaro Castle.

MALAGA'S CULINARY SCENE

REST. JOSÉ CARLOS GARCÍA

Located at Málaga's port, this Michelin-starred restaurant offers a gastronomic experience that combines traditional Andalusian flavors with avant-garde techniques. The tasting menu is a journey through the region's best produce.
Website: www.restaurantejcg.com
Location: Puerto de Málaga, Plaza de la Capilla, 1, 29001 Málaga, Spain
Tip: Reservations are recommended, especially during peak seasons.

EL PIMPI

A historic bodega bar in the heart of Málaga, El Pimpi is known for its traditional Andalusian ambiance and tapas. The walls adorned with photos of celebrities and bullfighting memorabilia add to its charm. It's a favorite among locals and tourists alike.
Website: www.elpimpi.com/en/
Location: Calle Granada, 62, 29015 Málaga, Spain
Tip: Try their house wine and pair it with a selection of tapas. The terrace offers a great view of the Alcazaba.

MESÓN DE CERVANTES

A cozy eatery offering a modern twist on traditional Spanish dishes. The menu is diverse, with a focus on fresh, local ingredients. The fusion of flavors and presentation is a testament to the chef's creativity.
Website: www.elmesondecervantes.com/eng/index.html
Location: Calle Álamos, 11, 29012 Málaga, Spain
Tip: The flambéed cod and Iberian pork cheek are must-tries. Reservations are advisable.

CASA LOLA

A vibrant tapas bar that captures the essence of Málaga's culinary scene. With a vast array of tapas to choose from, it's a haven for food enthusiasts. The decor, with its traditional tiles and wooden barrels, adds to the authentic experience.
Website: www.facebook.com/casalolamalaga/
Location: Calle Granada, 46, 29015 Málaga, Spain
Tip: The fried aubergines with honey and the octopus salad are crowd favorites.

MALAGA'S CULINARY SCENE

ESPETOS

Espetos are sardines skewered on a stick and grilled over an open flame, usually on a boat filled with sand. This simple yet delicious dish is a summer favorite in Málaga, best enjoyed by the beach.

Tip: Pair it with a cold beer or a glass of white wine.

BIENMESABE

A traditional Andalusian dessert, Bienmesabe is made of ground almonds, sugar, honey, and egg yolk. Its name translates to "tastes good to me," and one bite will tell you why.

Tip: It's often served with a scoop of ice cream or a dollop of whipped cream.

MALAGA WINE

Málaga is renowned for its sweet wines, made primarily from the Pedro Ximénez and Moscatel grapes. These wines are perfect as a dessert wine or an aperitif.

Tip: Visit a local bodega to sample different varieties and learn about the winemaking process.

PORRA ANTEQUERANA

A cold tomato-based soup, similar to gazpacho but thicker. It's made with tomatoes, peppers, bread, garlic, and olive oil, and is often topped with hard-boiled eggs or jamón.

Tip: It's a refreshing dish, perfect for Málaga's hot summer days.

SHOPPING IN MALAGA

CALLE LARIOS

The main shopping street in Málaga, Calle Larios is lined with high-end boutiques, international brands, and local shops. This pedestrianized street is always bustling, making it not just a shopping destination but also a place to soak in the city's atmosphere.
Website: https://visita.malaga.eu/es/que-hacer/calle-marques-de-larios-p103588
Location: Calle Marqués de Larios, 29005 Málaga, Spain
Tip: Visit during the evening when the street is beautifully illuminated, and local performers often entertain the crowds.

MUELLE UNO

A modern shopping complex located at Málaga's port. Muelle Uno offers a mix of international brands, local boutiques, and dining options, all with a view of the sea and the city's skyline.
Website: www.muelleuno.com
Location: Paseo de la Farola, 29016 Málaga, Spain
Tip: After shopping, take a stroll along the promenade and enjoy the sunset over the Mediterranean.

ATARAZANAS MARKET

A historic market where locals come to buy fresh produce, meats, cheeses, and more. The building itself, with its Moorish architecture and stained glass, is a sight to behold. It's a great place to experience the local culture and flavors.
Website: www.andalucia.com/cities/malaga/ataranzas-market.htm
Location: Calle Atarazanas, 10, 29005 Málaga, Spain
Tip: Try some local specialties like olives, cured ham, and cheeses. The market is busiest in the mornings.

SHOPPING IN MALAGA

EL CORTE INGLÉS

Spain's largest department store chain, El Corte Inglés in Málaga offers everything from fashion and electronics to gourmet food and souvenirs. It's a one-stop-shop for all your needs.
Website: www.elcorteingles.es/centroscomerciales/es/eci/centros/centro-comercial-malaga
Location: Av. de Andalucía, 4-6, 29007 Málaga, Spain
Tip: The store often has seasonal sales, so keep an eye out for discounts.

LA CASA AMARILLA

A unique concept store that offers a curated selection of art, design, books, and more. La Casa Amarilla (The Yellow House) is a haven for art enthusiasts and those looking for unique souvenirs.
Website: https://lacasa-amarilla.es/
Location: Calle Santos, 7, 29005 Málaga, Spain
Tip: They often host art exhibitions and workshops, so check their events calendar.

AGATHA PARIS

A chic jewelry store offering trendy and elegant pieces. Agatha Paris in Málaga is the go-to place for fashion-forward accessories that won't break the bank.
Website: www.agatha.es/es_ES
Location: Av. de Andalucía, 4-6 29007 MALAGA inside El Corte Inglés Málaga
Tip: Look for their signature Scottie dog designs, which are popular among locals and tourists alike.

FAMILY-FRIENDLY ACTIVITIES IN MALAGA

MÁLAGA BOTANICAL GARDEN

A tropical paradise located just outside the city center, the Málaga Botanical Garden is home to over 2,000 species of plants. The garden offers themed routes, including the Around the World in 80 Trees route, making it both educational and fun for kids.
Website:
https://laconcepcion.malaga.eu/en/
Location: Camino del Jardín Botánico, 3, 29014 Málaga, Spain
Tip: Don't miss the historical garden, which boasts plants from five continents.

INTERACTIVE MUSIC MUSEUM (MIMMA)

MIMMA - this unique space invites visitors to embark on a journey through the rich tapestry of global music. Children are encouraged to touch, play, and immerse themselves in a world of sound, exploring instruments from distant cultures and eras. The museum's hands-on approach, combined with its diverse collection and interactive exhibits, makes it a favorite among families. Engaging workshops and dedicated play areas further enhance the experience, ensuring that every visit to MIMMA is both educational and entertaining.
Website: www.musicaenaccion.com/en/
Location: Calle Beatas, 15, 29008 Málaga, Spain
Tip: Don't miss the opportunity to join one of their musical workshops where kids can discover and learn to play a new instrument in a fun environment.

CROCODILE PARK TORREMOLINOS

A thrilling adventure awaits families at the Crocodile Park Torremolinos, just a stone's throw away from Málaga. This unique park, spread over a vast area, is a sanctuary for over 200 crocodiles, ranging from tiny hatchlings to massive adults. As children gaze in wonder at these ancient reptiles, they can witness the excitement of live feeding sessions, feel the texture of a baby crocodile's skin, and delve deep into the world of crocodiles through informative guided tours.

The park's dedicated staff are passionate about educating visitors on the conservation and biology of these magnificent creatures. Beyond the crocodiles, the park's mini-zoo showcases a variety of other animals, ensuring a comprehensive and engaging experience for all.
Website: www.cocodrilospark.com
Location: Calle Cuba, 14, 29620 Torremolinos, Málaga, Spain
Tip: After exploring the crocodile habitats, take some time to visit the mini-zoo section to meet and learn about other intriguing animals.

FAMILY-FRIENDLY ACTIVITIES IN MALAGA

BIOPARC FUENGIROLA

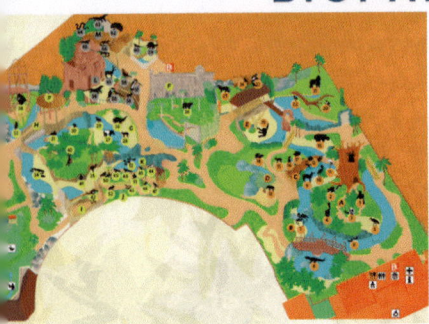

A short drive from Málaga, Bioparc Fuengirola is a modern zoo designed under the concept of "zoo-immersion". Here, families can embark on a journey through naturalistic habitats that recreate the jungles of Southeast Asia, the islands of the Indo-Pacific, Madagascar, and the forests of Equatorial Africa. The park is dedicated to the conservation of tropical species and offers an immersive experience where visitors can observe animals in environments that mirror their natural habitats. From tigers and gorillas to exotic birds and reptiles, the diversity of wildlife is astounding. Interactive exhibits and educational programs make it a perfect destination for kids to learn while having fun.

Website: www.bioparcfuengirola.es
Location: Av. Camilo José Cela, 6, 29640 Fuengirola, Málaga, Spain
Tip: Don't miss the daily animal feeding sessions and the opportunity to learn more about the park's conservation efforts.

SEA LIFE BENALMÁDENA

Dive into the mesmerizing underwater world at Sea Life Benalmádena. This state-of-the-art aquarium showcases a diverse range of marine life, from vibrant tropical fish and delicate seahorses to imposing sharks and graceful rays. Children are particularly enchanted by the interactive touch pool, where they can gently feel starfish and crabs, gaining a tactile understanding of marine biology. With themed zones and informative displays, it's an educational and fun-filled adventure for the whole family.

Website: www.visitsealife.com/benalmadena/en/
Location: Puerto Marina, s/n, 29630 Benalmádena, Málaga, Spain
Tip: Don't miss the scheduled feeding demonstrations, with the ray feeding session being a highlight for many visitors.

AUTOMOBILE AND FASHION MUSEUM

A unique museum that combines the worlds of cars and fashion. Families can explore a collection of vintage cars while also admiring fashion pieces from different eras. The interactive exhibits make it engaging for kids.

Website: https://museoautomovilmalaga.com/
Location: Av de Sor Teresa Prat, 15, 29003 Málaga, Spain
Tip: Check out the "Electricity" section, which showcases electric cars from the early 20th century.

MALAGA BY NIGHT

ILLUMINATED MONUMENTS AND EVENING STROLLS

MÁLAGA CATHEDRAL

The majestic Málaga Cathedral, also known as "La Manquita," is a sight to behold when illuminated at night. The intricate details of its architecture come alive, making it a perfect spot for an evening stroll.
Website: www.malagacatedral.com
Location: Calle Molina Lario, 9, 29015 Málaga, Spain
Tip: The surrounding plaza is filled with cafes and restaurants, ideal for a relaxing evening.

ALCAZABA OF MÁLAGA

This Moorish fortress, perched on a hill, offers panoramic views of the city lights. The ancient walls and gardens are beautifully lit, providing a romantic ambiance.
Website: www.andalucia.org/en/malaga-visitas-alcazaba-de-malaga
Location: Calle Alcazabilla, 2, 29012 Málaga, Spain
Tip: Combine your visit with the Roman Theatre located just below the Alcazaba.

PALMERAL DE LAS SORPRESAS

A modern promenade by the port, Palmeral de las Sorpresas is adorned with illuminated fountains and sculptures. The sea breeze and the city lights make it a popular spot for evening walks.
Website: www.puertomalaga.com/es/
Location: Muelle Dos, 29001 Málaga, Spain
Tip: There are several eateries along the promenade, perfect for a night-time snack.

BARS AND PUBS

CENTRAL BEER

A haven for craft beer enthusiasts, Central Beer offers a wide selection of local and international brews. The cozy ambiance and knowledgeable staff make it a favorite among locals.

Website: www.centralbeers.com
Location: Calle Cárcer, 6, 29012 Málaga, Spain
Tip: Try their tasting platter to sample a variety of beers.

EL PIMPI

A historic bar with traditional Andalusian decor, El Pimpi is known for its wines and tapas. The large terraces offer views of the Alcazaba and Roman Theatre.

Website: www.elpimpi.com/en/
Location: Calle Granada, 62, 29015 Málaga, Spain
Tip: Don't miss their signature sweet wine.

LA TRANCA

A vibrant bar with retro decor, La Tranca offers a lively atmosphere with Spanish music from the 80s and 90s. Their tapas and montaditos are a hit among patrons.

Website: http://www.latranca.es/
Location: Calle Carretería, 93, 29008 Málaga, Spain
Tip: The croquettes are a must-try.

MALAGA BY NIGHT

NIGHTCLUBS AND DANCE CLUBS

SALA GOLD

Sala Gold is one of Málaga's premier nightclubs, known for its opulent interiors and energetic dance floors. The club frequently hosts renowned DJs, ensuring a night of non-stop dancing and entertainment. With its state-of-the-art sound system and mesmerizing light shows, it's a must-visit for those looking to experience Málaga's vibrant nightlife.
Website: http://discotecasenmalaga.es/
Location: Calle Luis de Velázquez, 5, 29008 Málaga, Spain
Tip: Arrive early to avoid long queues, especially on weekends.

DISCOTHEQUE ANDÉN

One of Málaga's most iconic nightclubs, Discotheque Andén has been setting the city's nightlife pulse racing for decades.The club frequently hosts renowned DJs, ensuring a fresh and energetic playlist that keeps the crowd moving. Whether you're into house, techno, or the latest chart-toppers, Andén has something for every music enthusiast.
Website: https://discotecaanden.com/
Location: Plaza de Uncibay, 8, 29008 Málaga, Spain
Tip: Arrive early on weekends to avoid the queues and secure a good spot on the dance floor.

BUBBLES LOUNGE CLUB

Situated near the Málaga Marina, Bubbles Lounge Club offers a chic and sophisticated setting for night revelers. The club boasts an extensive cocktail menu, plush seating areas, and panoramic views of the port. The ambiance transitions from a relaxed lounge in the early evening to a pulsating dance club as the night progresses.
Website: www.facebook.com/Salabubbles/
Location: C. Mártires, 14, 29008 Málaga, Spain
Tip: The rooftop terrace is a perfect spot to enjoy the sea breeze and city views.

MALAGA BY NIGHT

LATE-NIGHT DINING

TABERNA UVEDOBLE

Located in the heart of Málaga, Taberna Uvedoble is a gem for those seeking late-night gourmet tapas in a cozy setting. With a modern twist on traditional Spanish dishes, the menu boasts a variety of flavors that cater to both classic and contemporary palates. The warm wooden interiors and ambient lighting create an inviting atmosphere, perfect for unwinding after a day of exploring.
Website: www.uvedobletaberna.com
Location: C/ Alcazabilla, 1, 29015 Málaga, Spain
Tip: Pair your tapas with their extensive selection of local wines for a complete dining experience.

RESTAURANT E VINO MÍO

Located next to the Cervantes Theatre, Vino Mío offers a diverse menu that caters to both traditional and contemporary tastes. Their late-night hours make it a favorite among theater-goers and night owls alike. The restaurant also features live flamenco performances, adding a touch of Spanish flair to your dining experience.
Website: https://restaurantevinomio.es/
Location: Plaza Jerónimo Cuervo, 2, 29012 Málaga, Spain
Tip: Try their fusion dishes, which combine classic Spanish ingredients with international flavors.

MESÓN MARIANO

Mesón Mariano is a hidden gem in Málaga's culinary scene. Open until midnight, this restaurant specializes in traditional Malagueño dishes prepared with a modern twist. The warm and cozy ambiance, combined with impeccable service, ensures a memorable late-night dining experience.
Website: www.facebook.com/profile.php?id=100063522493680
Location: Calle Granados, 2, 29008 Málaga, Spain
Tip: The "plato de los montes" is a hearty dish that's perfect for satisfying late-night hunger pangs.

MALAGA BY NIGHT

NIGHTLIFE AREAS

LA MALAGUETA

La Malagueta is not just a famous beach but also a buzzing nightlife hub. As the sun sets, the beachfront comes alive with numerous chiringuitos (beach bars) and clubs. The sea breeze, combined with lively music and the sound of waves, creates a unique atmosphere that's perfect for a night out.
Location: Paseo de Reding, 29016 Málaga, Spain
Tip: Enjoy a cocktail at one of the beach bars while soaking in the panoramic views of the Mediterranean.
the photo was taken on Noche de San Juan (The night of San Juan) happening on the 23rd of June

PLAZA DE LA MERCED

A historic square by day, Plaza de la Merced transforms into a vibrant nightlife spot as night falls. Surrounded by numerous bars, restaurants, and tapas joints, it's a favorite among locals and tourists alike. The square is also famous as the birthplace of Pablo Picasso, adding a touch of art and history to your night out.
Location: Plaza de la Merced, 29012 Málaga, Spain
Tip: Visit the Picasso statue in the square and then head to one of the nearby rooftop bars for a bird's-eye view of Málaga.

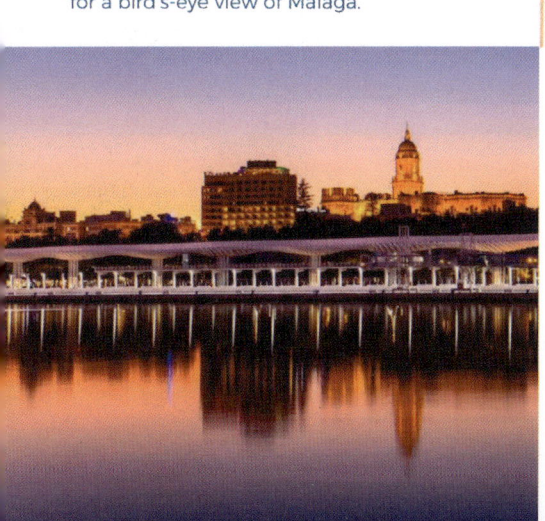

MUELLE UNO

Muelle Uno is Málaga's modern port area, boasting a mix of shopping, dining, and nightlife options. The promenade is lined with chic bars and restaurants offering everything from seafood to international cuisines. With its contemporary vibe and stunning views of the Alcazaba and Gibralfaro Castle, it's a must-visit for those looking to experience Málaga's modern side.
Website: www.muelleuno.com
Location: Paseo del Muelle Uno, 29016 Málaga, Spain
Tip: Take a leisurely stroll along the promenade, stopping at various establishments to sample their offerings and enjoy the ambiance.

SAFETY TIPS

- Be aware of your surroundings and keep an eye on your belongings, as pickpocketing can be an issue in crowded areas.
- Stick to well-lit streets and avoid wandering into unfamiliar, poorly lit areas late at night.
- Use reputable taxi services or ride-sharing apps to get around at night, especially if you are unfamiliar with the area. **Tip:** Save the phone number of a trusted taxi company in your phone for convenience.
- When enjoying the vibrant nightlife, always keep your drink in sight and never accept drinks from strangers. **Tip:** Drinking responsibly and staying hydrated will help ensure a safer and more enjoyable night out.
- Keep emergency contact numbers handy, including local police and your country's embassy.
- Carry a photocopy of your passport and other important documents, leaving the originals in a safe place.

By following these tips and exploring the city by night, you'll be able to experience the magic and charm of the city while staying safe and having an unforgettable time.

ART AND CULTURE IN MALAGA

MUSEO DEL PATRIMONIO MUNICIPAL

Situated in the heart of the city, the Museo del Patrimonio Municipal offers a deep dive into Málaga's rich cultural and historical tapestry. Spanning from ancient times to the modern era, the museum showcases a diverse collection of artifacts, paintings, and sculptures that tell the story of Málaga's evolution. The beautifully curated exhibits provide insights into the city's artistic, social, and economic development, making it a must-visit for history buffs and art enthusiasts alike.
Website: https://museodelpatrimoniomunicipal.malaga.eu/
Location: Paseo de Reding, 1, 29016 Málaga, Spain
Tip: The museum frequently hosts temporary exhibitions, so check their schedule for any special displays during your visit.

MALAGA WINE MUSEUM

Delve into the rich viticultural heritage of Málaga at the Malaga Wine Museum. Situated in the historic Palacio de Biedmas, the museum offers an immersive experience into the world of Andalusian wines. Discover the age-old traditions of winemaking, explore the different varieties of local grapes, and understand the nuances that make Málaga wines distinct. Interactive displays, vintage artifacts, and sensory experiences make it a treat for both connoisseurs and novices.
Website: www.andalucia.com/cities/malaga/museums/vino.htm
Location: Plaza de los Viñeros, 1, 29008 Málaga, Spain
Tip: Conclude your visit with a wine tasting session, where you can savor the flavors of the region's finest wines.

MUSEUM OF GLASS AND CRYSTAL

Nestled in a restored 18th-century palace, the Museum of Glass and Crystal is a shimmering testament to the art of glassmaking. Boasting a collection of over 3,000 pieces, the museum takes visitors on a journey through the history of glass, from ancient Egyptian artifacts to contemporary art pieces. Each room is meticulously designed to reflect different historical periods, enhancing the overall experience. The passionate guides and the intimate setting make it a unique cultural gem in Málaga.
Website: www.museovidrioycristalmalaga.com
Location: Plazuela Santísimo Cristo de la Sangre, 2, 29012 Málaga, Spain
Tip: Don't miss the stunning stained glass displays, which are a highlight of the museum's collection.

ART AND CULTURE IN MALAGA

CAC MALAGA CONTEMPORARY ART MUSEUM

A hub of modern artistic expression, the CAC Malaga Contemporary Art Museum stands as a testament to the city's vibrant contemporary art scene. Housed in a former wholesale market, the museum showcases a dynamic collection of works from both international and Spanish artists. From avant-garde installations to thought-provoking paintings, the exhibits challenge perceptions and inspire creativity. Regularly rotating exhibitions ensure there's always something new to explore.
Website: www.cacmalaga.eu
Location: Calle Alemania, s/n, 29001 Málaga, Spain
Tip: The museum frequently hosts workshops and lectures, making it a lively center for artistic discourse and learning.

RUSSIAN MUSEUM COLLECTION ST. PETERSBURG

A branch of the State Russian Museum in St. Petersburg, this institution in Málaga offers a fascinating glimpse into Russian art and culture. The museum showcases a diverse range of artworks, from ancient icons to avant-garde pieces. The exhibitions rotate regularly, ensuring there's always something new to discover.
Website: www.coleccionmuseoruso.es
Location: Av. Sor Teresa Prat, No. 15, 29003 Málaga, Spain
Tip: The museum's audio guide provides rich context and background to the artworks. It's worth investing in for a deeper understanding of the exhibits.

ART AND CULTURE IN MALAGA

CENTRE POMPIDOU MÁLAGA

An offshoot of the famous Parisian museum, the Centre Pompidou Málaga is a beacon of contemporary art in the city. Housed in a strikingly modern building with a multicolored cube structure, it showcases a rotating selection of works from the main Pompidou collection. The exhibitions span various mediums, from painting and sculpture to video art.
Website: www.centrepompidou-malaga.eu
Location: Pasaje Doctor Carrillo Casaux, s/n, Muelle 1, 29016 Málaga, Spain
Tip: The museum offers free entry on Sundays in the last couple of hours before closing. It's a great time to explore without the usual crowds.

MUSEO JORGE RANDO

Dedicated to the works of the expressionist artist Jorge Rando, this museum is a testament to the power of raw emotion in art. Rando's works, characterized by their intense colors and bold strokes, delve deep into themes of suffering, spirituality, and nature. The museum itself is set in a refurbished monastery, adding to its unique charm.
Website: www.museojorgerando.org
Location: Calle Cruz del Molinillo, 12, 29013 Málaga, Spain
Tip: The museum frequently hosts art workshops and lectures. Check their events calendar to catch one during your visit.

REVELLO DE TORO MUSEUM

Dedicated to the works of the acclaimed Spanish portraitist Félix Revello de Toro, this museum is a must-visit for art enthusiasts. Housed in a 17th-century building, it showcases over 100 works by the artist, capturing the essence of his subjects with incredible precision and sensitivity.
Website: www.museorevellodetoro.net/en/
Location: Calle Afligidos, 5, 29015 Málaga, Spain
Tip: The museum is located in Málaga's historic center, making it a convenient stop as you explore the city's ancient streets and landmarks.

ARCHITECTURAL LANDMARKS IN MALAGA

SACRED HEART CHURCH

The Sacred Heart Church, locally known as Sagrado Corazon, is a stunning example of neo-Gothic architecture in Málaga. With its intricate stained glass windows, soaring spires, and detailed sculptures, the church is a serene oasis in the heart of the city. The interiors, adorned with beautiful frescoes and wooden carvings, exude a sense of tranquility and devotion.
Website: https://visita.malaga.eu/en/what-to-see-and-do/culture/historic-monuments/churches-and-chapels/sagrado-corazon-church-p104032
Location: Pl. de San Ignacio, s/n, 29008 Málaga, Spain
Tip: The evening mass, with its melodious hymns, offers a soulful experience, even for non-religious visitors.

SANTA MARÍA DE LA VICTORIA BASILICA

Santa María de la Victoria Basilica stands as a beacon of Málaga's rich religious and architectural heritage. This majestic basilica, with its Baroque façade and ornate interiors, is a testament to the city's devotion and artistry. Inside, visitors are greeted by intricate frescoes, gilded altars, and a revered image of the Virgin of Victory. The crypt and the side chapels further add to the basilica's historical significance, making it a must-visit for history enthusiasts and spiritual seekers alike.
Website: https://visita.malaga.eu/en/what-to-see-and-do/culture/historic-monuments/monuments/santa-maria-de-la-victoria-basilica-p103582
Location: Plaza Santuario, 29012 Málaga, Spain
Tip: The guided tours offer a deep dive into the basilica's history and the legends associated with it. Ensure to check the timings before visiting.

TRADE FAIR AND CONGRESS IN MÁLAGA

The Palacio de Ferias y Congresos de Málaga is a modern architectural marvel, serving as the city's primary venue for trade fairs, exhibitions, and conventions. With its state-of-the-art facilities and sleek design, it plays a pivotal role in Málaga's business and cultural events. The complex is equipped with spacious halls, auditoriums, and meeting rooms, making it a hub of activity throughout the year.
Website: www.fycma.com
Location: Av. de José Ortega y Gasset, 201, 29006 Málaga, Spain
Tip: Check their events calendar before visiting; you might stumble upon an interesting exhibition or trade fair.

ARCHITECTURAL LANDMARKS IN MALAGA

LA FAROLA DE MALAGA

La Farola de Malaga, or the Lighthouse of Malaga, is an iconic landmark that has stood guard over the city's port for over two centuries. With its elegant design and strategic location, it offers panoramic views of the Mediterranean Sea and the city skyline. As one of the few female-named lighthouses in Spain, La Farola holds a special place in the hearts of locals.
Website: www.puertomalaga.com/es/la-farola/
Location: Paseo del Muelle Uno, 29016 Málaga, Spain
Tip: The area around the lighthouse is perfect for a leisurely evening stroll, with the backdrop of the setting sun.

ALCAZABA OF MÁLAGA

Perched atop a hill overlooking the city, the Alcazaba is a palatial fortification that dates back to the 11th century. It's a testament to Málaga's Moorish history, with its intricate archways, lush gardens, and panoramic views of the port. The fortress seamlessly blends Roman and Islamic architectural styles.
Website: www.alcazabaygibralfaro.malaga.eu/en
Location: Calle Alcazabilla, 2, 29012 Málaga, Spain
Tip: Combine your visit with the nearby Roman Theatre and Gibralfaro Castle for a comprehensive historical experience.

GIBRALFARO CASTLE

This iconic castle stands majestically on Mount Gibralfaro, offering breathtaking views of Málaga and the Mediterranean Sea. Originally built in the 10th century, the castle has witnessed numerous battles and sieges, most notably during the Reconquista.
Website:
https://alcazabaygibralfaro.malaga.eu/en/index.html
Location: Camino Gibralfaro, s/n, 29016 Málaga, Spain
Tip: Wear comfortable shoes as the climb to the castle can be steep. The sunset views from the castle walls are particularly stunning.

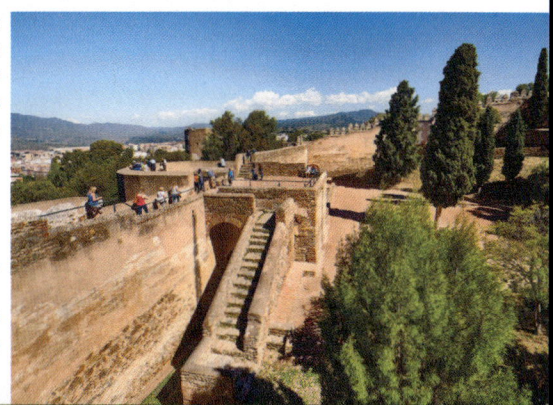

ARCHITECTURAL LANDMARKS IN MALAGA

TEATRO ROMANO (ROMAN THEATRE)

Located at the foot of the Alcazaba fortress, the Roman Theatre is a testament to Málaga's ancient history. Dating back to the 1st century BC, it is the oldest monument in the city. Over the centuries, the theatre was buried and forgotten, only to be rediscovered in the 1950s. Today, it has been restored and occasionally hosts performances.

Website: www.juntadeandalucia.es/cultura/enclaves/enclave-arqueologico-teatro-romano-de-malaga
Location: Calle Alcazabilla, s/n, 29015 Málaga, Spain
Tip: Combine your visit with the nearby Alcazaba for a deep dive into Málaga's rich history. The interpretative center offers insightful information about the theatre's history and architecture.

MÁLAGA CATHEDRAL

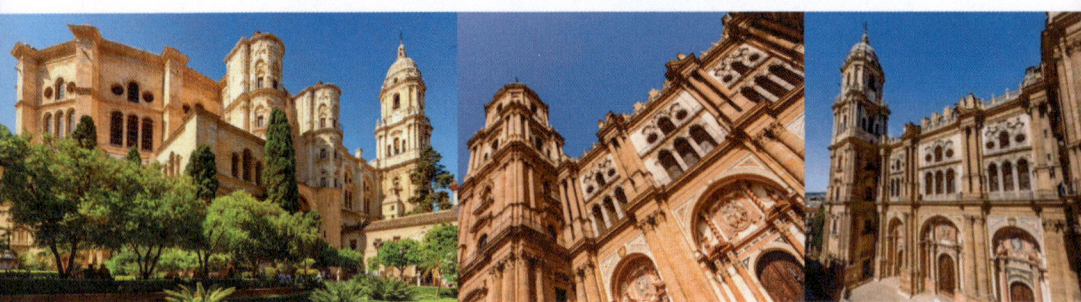

Known locally as "La Manquita" or "The One-Armed Lady" due to its unfinished second tower, Málaga Cathedral is a beautiful example of Renaissance architecture. Inside, visitors can admire the intricate choir stalls, grand organ, and various chapels adorned with religious art.

Website: www.malagacatedral.com
Location: Calle Molina Lario, 9, 29015 Málaga, Spain
Tip: For a small fee, you can access the rooftop and enjoy panoramic views of the city.

PALACIO DE LA ADUANA

This neoclassical building, constructed in the late 18th century, once served as a customs house. Today, it houses the Museum of Málaga, showcasing the city's archaeological and fine arts collections. The museum's exhibits trace the region's history from prehistoric times to the 20th century, with artifacts, paintings, and sculptures on display.

Website:
www.museosdeandalucia.es/web/museodemalaga/informacion-general
Location: Plaza de la Aduana, s/n, 29015 Málaga, Spain
Tip: The museum offers free admission to EU citizens. Allocate at least a couple of hours to explore its vast collections.

DAY TRIPS FROM MALAGA

RONDA

Perched atop a deep gorge, Ronda offers breathtaking views, historic bridges, and a rich history. The town is known for its bullring, old town, and the dramatic El Tajo gorge.
Location: Ronda, Spain. Distance: Approximately 100 km from Málaga.
Tip: Walk across the Puente Nuevo bridge for a stunning view of the gorge below.

NERJA

Known for its stunning beaches and the Caves of Nerja, this coastal town is a must-visit. The Balcony of Europe offers panoramic views of the Mediterranean Sea.
Location: Nerja, Spain. Distance: Approximately 70 km from Málaga.
Tip: Visit the Nerja Caves to see impressive stalactites and stalagmites.

ANTEQUERA

A historic city featuring ancient dolmens, a Moorish fortress, and beautiful churches. Nearby, El Torcal Natural Park offers unique limestone formations.
Location: Antequera, Spain. Distance: About 55 km from Málaga.
Tip: Don't miss the Dolmens of Antequera, a UNESCO World Heritage site.

FRIGILIANA

A charming white village located in the hills above Nerja, Frigiliana is known for its narrow, winding streets and Moorish architecture.
Location: Frigiliana, Spain. Distance: Approximately 76 km from Málaga.
Tip: Try the local honey and explore the village's artisan shops.

MARBELLA

A luxurious resort town known for its beautiful beaches, historic old town, and vibrant nightlife. The Puerto Banús marina is a hub for high-end shopping and dining.
Location: Marbella, Spain. Distance: About 60 km from Málaga.
Tip: Stroll along the Golden Mile, lined with luxury boutiques and beachfront villas.

DAY TRIPS FROM MALAGA

MIJAS

A picturesque white village nestled in the mountains, Mijas offers panoramic views of the coast, traditional Andalusian charm, and a famous donkey taxi service.
Location: Mijas, Spain. Distance: Approximately 30 km from Málaga.
Tip: Visit the Mijas Bullring and the Church of Immaculate Conception.

GIBRALTAR

A British Overseas Territory known for the iconic Rock of Gibraltar, its unique mix of cultures, and the famous Barbary macaques.
Location: Gibraltar. Distance: About 120 km from Málaga.
Tip: Explore St. Michael's Cave and take a cable car to the top of the Rock for panoramic views.

TARIFA

The southernmost point of mainland Europe, Tarifa is a haven for windsurfers and kitesurfers. Its beaches are pristine, and the town has a laid-back vibe.
Location: Tarifa, Spain. Distance: Approximately 160 km from Málaga.
Tip: Visit the Castle of Guzmán el Bueno and enjoy fresh seafood at local restaurants.

AXARQUÍA

A region known for its white villages, vineyards, and olive groves. The landscape is dotted with almond and fig trees, making it a scenic destination.
Location: Axarquía, Spain. Distance: Varies depending on the village, but generally within 50-80 km from Málaga.
Tip: Explore villages like Comares, Cómpeta, and Canillas de Aceituno.

SIERRA DE LAS NIEVES NATIONAL PARK

A UNESCO Biosphere Reserve, this park is home to diverse flora and fauna, including the rare Spanish fir tree. It's ideal for hiking and nature enthusiasts.
Location: Sierra de las Nieves, Spain. Distance: Approximately 90 km from Málaga.
Tip: Visit the Torrecilla peak, the highest point in the park, for stunning views.

END NOTE

Málaga, with its rich history, vibrant culture, and stunning coastal views, offers a unique blend of traditional and modern experiences. From the ancient Alcazaba fortress to the contemporary art of the Pompidou Centre, there's something for every traveler in this sun-soaked city. As you wander through its narrow streets, indulge in local delicacies, and soak up the Andalusian sun, you'll discover the true essence of Málaga. Whether you're here for a weekend getaway or an extended stay, Málaga promises unforgettable memories.

Enjoy your journey in this Mediterranean gem!

Unlock a world of unforgettable experiences with Tailored Travel Guides! As your go-to source for personalized and meticulously crafted travel guides, we ensure that every adventure is uniquely yours. Our team of dedicated travel experts and local insiders design each guide with your preferences, interests, and travel style in mind, providing you with the ultimate customized travel experience. Embark on your next journey with confidence, knowing that Tailored Travel Guides has got you covered. To explore more exceptional destinations and discover a treasure trove of additional guides, visit www.tailoredtravelguides.com. or our collection available
on **Amazon** at this link: www.amazon.com/stores/Tailored-Travel-Guides/author/B0C4TV5TZX or
on **Google Play**, at this link: https://play.google.com/store/books/author?id=Tailored+Travel+Guides
on **Etsy**, at this link: https://tailoredtravelguides.etsy.com

Happy travels, and here's to a lifetime of remarkable memories!

Join our Tailored Travel Guides Network for more benefits by accessing this link:
https://mailchi.mp/d151cba349e8/ttgnetwork
Or by scanning the QR code

Loved Your Journey With Our Guide? 🌟
Your feedback makes a world of difference! If our guide helped you explore or enjoy your destination, we would be thrilled if you could take a moment to leave us a 5-star review on our product page.🙏
Simply click the link or go to any of our product pages on your preferred retailer website and **share your recommendations.**
https://www.amazon.com/stores/Tailored-Travel-Guides/author/B0C4TV5TZX

Thank you for chosing Tailored Travel Guides!

Discover your journey!

CHECK OUT THE ITALY UNCOVERED SERIES

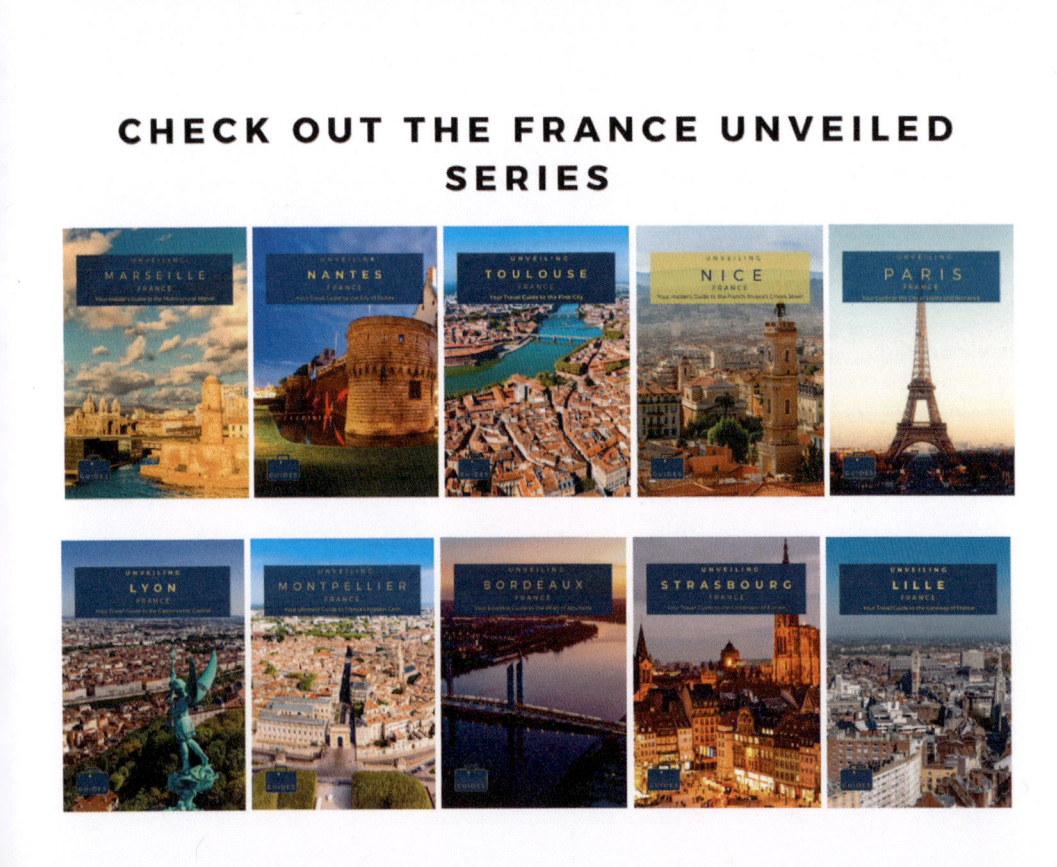

CHECK OUT THE FRANCE UNVEILED SERIES

Printed in Great Britain
by Amazon